Toddler Discipline

The Parent's Guide to raising your toddler with the positive discipline. How to Eliminate Tantrums and Help your Toddler to Grow in Capable and Confident

Kate Cartes

© **Copyright 2021 By Kate Cartes- All rights reserved.**

The content contained within this book may not be reproduced, duplicated or transmitted without direct written permission from the author or the publisher.

Under no circumstances will any blame or legal responsibility be held against the publisher, or author, for any damages, reparation, or monetary loss due to the information contained within this book. Either directly or indirectly.

Legal Notice:

This book is copyright protected. This book is only for personal use. You cannot amend, distribute, sell, use, quote or paraphrase any part, or the content within this book, without the consent of the author or publisher.

Disclaimer Notice:

Please note the information contained within this document is for educational and entertainment purposes only. All effort has been executed to present accurate, up to date, and reliable, complete information. No warranties of any kind are declared or implied. Readers acknowledge that the author is not engaging in the rendering of legal, financial, medical or professional advice. The content within this book has been derived from various sources. Please consult a licensed professional before attempting any techniques outlined in this book.

By reading this document, the reader agrees that under no circumstances is the author responsible for any losses, direct or indirect, which are incurred as a result of the use of information contained within this document, including, but not limited to, errors, omissions, or inaccuracies.

Table of Contents

Introduction 6
CHAPTER 1: Conflict Management 10
   Conflicts Can Ruin Relationships 11
   What Battles Are Worth Fighting and What Are Not? 13
   A Messy Room 13
   Eating Times and Habits 14
   The Fight List 14
   Skills You Need to Pick Your Battles Wisely 15
   How to Communicate Well 17
CHAPTER 2: Focus On Solution 22
   A. Positive Communication 23
   Ways to Build-up the Child's Self-esteem 27
   The Problem-Solving Approach 28
CHAPTER 3: Using Encouragement Effectively 38
   Encouragement vs. Praise 39
CHAPTER 4: Listen 46
   Getting Down on Their Level, Eye-To-Eye Conversations 47
   Listening and Responding Appropriately 48
   Asking Questions and Respecting Answers 49
   Positive Language and Positive Discipline 50
   Emotional Learning 53
CHAPTER 5: Pay Attention 56
   When your Child Needs Special help 56
   Unable to Focus 57
   Having Sleep Issues 57

Health Is Not On a Good Note 57

Unable to Express 58

Mixed Feelings of Anger, Excitement, and Sorrow 58

Growing as a Family: Finding Support, Resources, and Sanity 59

Your Support Is the Key... 60

Hit the Help Resources 61

Medical Attention 61

Additional Attention 62

Discussion and Debate 62

Educational Grooming 63

Getting Study Kits.. 63

Understand the Variation 63

Explore the Options 64

Match Interests... 64

Participate to Make It Rational 65

Boost Your Kid's Confidence 65

CHAPTER 6: The Listening Process 66

Chinese Whispers.. 70

Why Is It Helpful to Understand This Process? 71

A Positive Listening Attitude 72

What Is an Active Listener?... 73

CHAPTER 7: Act Without Words: The Secret of Staying Calm 74

Mindful Hugging.. 79

CHAPTER 8: Bad Words 84

CHAPTER 9: Handling Tantrums 92

Stress Tantrums 92

Manipulative Tantrums.. 94

Communication Tantrums 96

What to Do During Tantrums 97

CHAPTER 10: How to Replace Punishment with Positive Parenting **100**

Tips and Solutions for Peaceful and Positive Parenting 106

Conclusion **108**

Introduction

Positive discipline is a natural teaching tool that is based on three simple steps: Positive reinforcement, positive direction, and positive guidance. It teaches children to make better choices and can help them develop successful habits over the long term. People who implement positive discipline regularly have better relationships with their children and enjoy a closer bond. No matter how old you are, positive discipline can benefit your entire family. We believe that parents and schools are more effective when they apply positive discipline. With positive discipline, you teach your kids the way they should behave. You want your kids to learn from their mistakes and to make good decisions.

Positive discipline works for all ages of children, including preschoolers.

Positive Discipline is a proven method that has helped millions of families. It lowers the incidence of discipline problems in children while increasing levels of cooperation and self-esteem. This tool will help you and your child learn how to have a rewarding relationship with each other. Positive Discipline in the classroom is a proven method of teaching that can be effective for almost any student.

The purpose of positive discipline is to introduce your child to the school environment and its rules. From this point on, you will consistently reinforce positive behavior throughout the school year, all while avoiding sanctions that don't always feel fair to your child.

You want to teach your child that he or she has responsibility for his or her actions. But you also need to make sure your child knows that he or she is not in any kind of trouble when you have a talk about positive behavior instead of negative behavior.

A positive discipline system does not mean you will no longer punish your child or even spank him or her. If you spank a child and then use positive discipline, the child will defiantly grow attached to the angry feelings he or she gets when the parent punishes him or her. It's important that the punishments are short and sweet so as not to create those emotional feelings.

Children come into being without instructions. It is up to parents to raise them properly, provide discipline, and ensure that they are well-provided. Every parent wants a well-behaved, happy, healthy, and respectful child. No one likes to raise spoiled brats, but sometimes children become too difficult to deal with, leaving parents frustrated and perplexed.

What will you do when your child becomes disrespectful and does not listen? Or deliberately defies or disobeys your request to behave.

As you encounter these problems, it is important to reinforce your role as a parent. You are the primary person who can provide a suitable discipline for your child and help him become self-reliant, self-controlled, and respectful. Other figures and authorities like therapists, relatives, and mentors can help, but the major responsibility rests on your shoulder.

CHAPTER 1:

Conflict Management

There are rare things that shake a parent's confidence in the way they are raising their kids. They don't question their parenting style unless their children start to exhibit bad behavior. They examine the shortcomings and challenges they still face but there is one problem—their kids are no longer kids.

They are grownups who have a mind of their own. They don't just listen to you and adhere to what you say.

They question. They counter your orders with their preferences. They refuse to do the things you tell them because they no longer need to be told what to do. The communication channels are also broken and no longer flow easily. It's like treading carefully into a field full of mines. The minute you take the wrong step, things blow up.

Conflicts Can Ruin Relationships

Conflicts between parents and teenagers are a common sight. With their hormones raging, teenagers often get so heated that they start to talk back, misbehave, or ignore their parents. They fight because they want to change their relationship with their parents. They have always been in the backseat of the car and now they want to be in the driver's seat. They want to live by their own rules and make decisions that concern themselves on their own. They want to be included in important discussions about the family instead of just agreeing to things mindlessly. They want to shake their parents into this new reality where they want them to see them as a new, more intellectual, and exciting person. They act over-dramatic, make mountains out of molehills, and try to push their parents into agreeing to things they are proposing.

They also want their parents to appreciate them for who they are becoming or have become even when it isn't a positive change. These quarrels, if not handled maturely, can lead to rifts between delicate relationships. For starters, it can disrupt the peace in the household and among siblings. It can also lead to blaming, shaming, and unraveling old grievances and past failures. It can make both the parent and the teenager feel misunderstood and hurt. It can lead to anger and abuse in rare cases where one or both the parties use physical or verbal abuse to hurt one another. Some teenagers have also left their homes and moved in with their partners or friends because they feel their parents don't see them for who they are, and they are done with all the fights and violence it leads to.

What Battles Are Worth Fighting and What Are Not?

Picking our battles means we critically analyze what arguments are worth stretching and what aren't. It involves thinking and deciding whether to go into action mode or not. It also means that we choose things with a profitable reward and leave the ones that pose no return on investment. As parents, we need to choose to either go into the fight or flight mood. There will always be some issues worth fighting over and some that aren't. Your goal is to identify the ones that are and hold your ground. As for the rest, you can choose to ignore it. To make things interesting, we have created a flight and fight list to help parents understand if they are picking up the right issues to fight over or not.

A Messy Room

Some kids can't stand a dirty room. Some don't have the time to clean their rooms. A messy room isn't something you want to deal with. They can be messy eaters and careless about how their room looks, as long as they can find something clean to wear to school. Therefore, being too aggressive about it won't do you or them any good. Let it be. They will learn to behave when they move into a place of their own and spend hours looking for something.

Eating Times and Habits

Some teenagers, especially girls, give their parents a hard time with their eating habits. They will start a new diet every other week and starve themselves. They will survive on detox cleanses that taste like vomit because they have to shed a few pounds for an upcoming event. For guys, you can find them standing by the fridge, eating anything they can find in the middle of the night, and then leave the kitchen a mess. Now, we do believe that healthy eating habits must be encouraged, but there are ways to go about it.

The Fight List

This list has the things you have to fight about if you see them not adhering to them. For example:

Paying Respect to Others

If they don't show others the respect that they deserve, they need to be confronted about it. It is never okay for them to be disrespectful towards their peers, parents, or teachers. They must not show prejudice toward someone or think of themselves as privileged in any way.

Curfews

They should comply with the rules and limitations set by you. Of course, there can be exceptions such as a class that ended late, a flat tire, or an urgent problem with a peer. They must still know to inform you about it.

Their Grades

There is no going around it. If their grades are poor, the reasons need to be deliberated in a calm yet stern manner. You can scold them for not completing their homework on time or not spending time preparing for their exams.

Skills You Need to Pick Your Battles Wisely

How can you pick your battles wisely and without creating a scene every time with your teenager? Below are some great skills to use to make the right choice.

Understand the Reasons for Arguments

The first thing you need to know is why you are fighting about something. Teenagers have different personalities and styles. Some teenagers just fight for the sake of arguing. Some are shy and avoid confrontation. Thus, knowing the reason for an argument combined with the personality of your child will help you pick the right battle worth fighting about.

What Are You Trying to Achieve?

What is it that you wish to achieve with the conflict? What is the outcome you want? Do you just want to prove them wrong and yourself right? If so, it isn't worth the fight. Or do they want to handle waywardness and leave a positive impact on their wellbeing if they choose to change? If so, it is a worthy cause.

Getting the Timing Right

Sometimes, we are fighting the right cause but choose an inappropriate time. Kids, when in a bad mood, won't listen to you, no matter how meaningful and rewarding the outcome could be. Therefore, if you want them to listen and obey, choose the right time to have an argument or discussion.

Can a Compromise Be Made?

Is it possible that the conflict ends on a positive note where both of you settle on the same thing? Demands can be negotiated and knowing how to negotiate can reduce the pressure on you. You want them to respect you and obey you. They want the same respect in return.

How to Communicate Well

Communication is a key element when raising a child. It is the easiest thing to do but is often the most neglected area of childcare.

Modern-day life doesn't give us a lot of free time and parents who are working alongside raising children often feel like there is even less time to relax, never mind finding time to sit and have a conversation. They become more involved in pursuing their own interests. This makes it even easier for the parent to use what little downtime they have to switch off and relax.

It is important that the parent takes this time to recharge their batteries, but by setting aside 15-30 minutes of that time each day to chat with their children, they can save themselves a lot of problems when their child reaches the teenage years. This time will become a natural part of your child's daily routine and they are less likely to become resentful of questions about their lives as they get older.

Sustaining this relaxed channel of communication throughout their early formative years will make it much easier for them to approach you when they do encounter a problem in their lives.

This process will also facilitate a parent should they need to broach a sensitive and potentially explosive subject with their children.

If possible, try to give each child a full hour to himself once a week for quality time. This can be anything from watching a movie to playing a game or even just going for a walk. During this hour keep your attention focused entirely on that child and what they want to do, to the exclusion of all else, (except emergencies). By doing this, you will further strengthen the child's belief that they can approach you with issues that are worrying them and you are giving them a window of opportunity to do this privately.

A child's mind is like a sponge and they will soak up everything around them but, unfortunately, they do not possess the necessary emotional ability and sense of reasoning to make sense of all of it.

Stress is not restricted to just adults and, in the same way, an adult's mind does, the child's mind can become overloaded, leading to confusion and ultimately, stress.

As adults, we understand stress but a child simply feels confused and overwhelmed which leads them to act out, throw tantrums and become tearful or withdrawn.

As a society, we naturally avoid answering questions about subjects that we believe the child is too young to discuss. The trick here is to always give an answer, but ensure it is age-appropriate and containing only as much information as absolutely necessary.

A refusal to answer leads the child to try to make sense of something on its own. With their limited life experience, this invariably leads to a negative conclusion.

Scenario:

Dad reaches the household from a demanding day at exertion and is taking his bad mood out on those around him. The child overhears their parents arguing and asks dad why mummy was shouting at him.

Response to a three-year-old child:

Because daddy was cheeky to mummy, but she told me off and I said sorry so she is not angry anymore.

By answering the child's question, the parent has recognized that the child is concerned and has answered in such a way that the situation has been understood. This has offered reassurance that mum and dad are ok. They also see the concept of acknowledging and apologizing for bad behavior being played out by the parent.

It is irrelevant that the argument was not about dad being cheeky as such; what is important is the fact the father gave a full answer to the question, but in a way, a 3-year-old child could relate to.

If the same scenario were based on an 8-year-old child, then the answer would require more detail. Not only has the 8-year-old got a better-developed sense of reasoning, but also, they are more astute due to the additional 5 years of life experience. In this case, the answer would be along the lines of:

I had a hard day at work so I feel very tired because I haven't had a chance to relax yet. This made me bad-tempered and I took it out on mum. It's ok though because she told me off and I realized I was behaving badly so I said sorry.

The result is the same as it was for the three-year-old, but by giving a more detailed account of the situation the older child had enough information to process it and accept it.

CHAPTER 2:

Focus On Solution

Focusing on solutions that demonstrate respect, reasonable, helpful, and problem-related is the best approach to resolve misbehavior. It is one of the foundations of successful family meetings, where children are involved in the process of establishing rules and consequences for behavioral issues. Communication is a vital key to find solutions. Positive and healthy two-way communication is vital to building his self-esteem and self-discipline. Children naturally thrive with praise and words of encouragement, but listening to them boosts their belief in themselves and makes them feel loved and worthy.

A. Positive Communication

Hearing the child utters his first word is a delightful moment for parents. You anticipate the next words and phrases that he is going to say, feeling proud every time he calls you mom or dad. As your child grows, his language development and communication skills evolve. He learns to express his needs, feelings, and thoughts.

Communicating with a Baby

The baby's brain is naturally "hard-wired" to the sound of a human voice. He responds using his body language, facial expressions, and noises. To encourage his language development, you need to understand and listen to what he wants to express:

- **Crying**. It is his primary method of communication.

- **Attend to his needs** when he begins to cry, to let him know that you understand and acknowledge his message.

- **Talk** to him frequently about anything or read baby books. He loves hearing your voice and having your presence.

- **Listen** to his noise-making or cooing. Look him in the eye and encourage him to smile or talk.

Communicating with a Toddler

Toddlers begin to string words and utter simple sentences using more than a hundred vocabulary words. Encourage your child's language development with the following:

- Answer his questions using simple language.
- Allow him to finish what he wants to say.
- Spend some time every day just talking with him.
- Listen attentively to what he is saying, instead of correcting his grammar.
- Avoid showing impatient body language like foot-tapping, sighing, or eye-rolling. It will discourage him from sharing his feelings or thoughts.
- Squat down on his level and maintain eye contact.
- Refrain from talking with him when you are walking away or your back is turned.
- Smile.
- Cuddle him often.
- Use a gentle tone of voice. Avoid yelling.
- Become aware that if the child is constantly interrupting adult conversations, he wants attention.

Communicating with Older Children

At this level, he has mastered his language ability and can convey clear ideas. He can alter his speech from casual to formal, depending on the circumstances and interactions. You can show your interest in what he wants to tell you by:

- Making time to listen to your child every day without any distractions. Have an exclusive, quality time with him to talk about anything that concerns him or just random topics that interest you both.

- Respect his point of view and encourage him to give a different opinion.

- Avoid lecturing, criticizing, or interrupting when he is telling you something.

- Ask open-ended questions that will prompt him to share and describe his experiences for the day.

Positive Phrases for Young Children

- Thanks for helping
- You did it!
- I like playing with you
- You are so thoughtful
- Good job
- That was a great try
- Nice idea!
- I am very proud of you

Establishing open, healthy, and positive communication in the family is empowering. It allows everyone, especially kids, to learn to listen and talk effectively. It is an essential key element of positive parenting, allowing children to express their concerns freely, without criticism and contempt.

Moreover, positive communication is the key to help you and your child focus on finding solutions that will make his journey to adulthood easier and more fulfilling. Helping your child understand, process, manage, and resolve conflict is a life skill, which becomes handy and useful in his everyday life.

It is essential to keep communication positive. How you respond creates an immediate impact and affect his mood. For instance, your child will start schooling, and you want him to be prepared mentally and emotionally, so you start sharing some tips and reminders. If you convey that school is fun and exciting because he can play and learn, meet new friends, and more, he will look forward to it. But if you project fears on him, the child will not be too keen to go to school and have a harder time adjusting to the new experience.

Ways to Build-up the Child's Self-esteem

- Use the words happy and encouraged regularly. "I feel very encouraged when you extend help to your brother." "I feel happy when you help me."

- For every negative, always accompany it with at least 3 positives.

- Speak to your kid as you would speak to adults.

- Use the sandwich approach when giving feedback.

- Notice when he is good using specific praise to reinforce the positive behavior.

- Let him know that you believe in his abilities.

- Praise the efforts and not just the results.

- Separate him from his behavior. Show that you disapprove the act, but not him. Say, "drawing on the wall is a naughty thing to do" rather than "you are such a naughty kid."

- Thank him when he helps you and initiates to do household chores.

- Tell your kid what you do want him to do instead of what you don't want.

- Never assume that he already knows how much you love him, tell him often.

The Problem-Solving Approach
1. Talk About the Child's Feelings and Needs

"I See That You Are Mad. Is It Because Your Brother Took Your Ball Without Asking You?"

These statements convey that you know your child's feelings even though he does not say them aloud. When you identify and recognize his feelings and needs, you are demonstrating that you understand why he is acting like that or why his behavior has changed.

Always remember to begin all corrections by reaffirming the connection. When children misbehave, they feel bad about the situation or themselves, so they disconnect. To reconnect, you can try these examples:

- Stoop down to his level and look him straight in the eye. "Pushing hurts, so no pushing. You can tell your brother, "Move, please."

- Make loving eye contact and say—"You are upset."

- Pick him up—"You want to play longer, but it is time to sleep."

- Put your hand on his shoulder—"You are afraid to tell me about the broken vase."

As a parent, it is your role to help your kid understand his feelings and needs. He needs you to show him how to manage his feelings in constructive and positive ways. Use age-appropriate language and get down to his eye level during the conversation. It shows respect and sincerity, which lets down his guard and become more communicative of his needs and feelings.

Kids, like adults, have their own share of complex feelings that excite, frighten, worry, or make them nervous, embarrassed, or jealous. But it is more difficult for them to express their feelings clearly because they have a limited vocabulary. So, they use other means to communicate with adults like facial expressions, body language, or misbehaviors. When their parents or caregivers cannot decipher what they want to communicate, children display inappropriate acts.

It is important to let your child know that you heard him loud and clear.

- Set a regular talk time and make sure that you give undivided attention to him during the conversation.

- Encourage him to share his feelings, thoughts, fears, dreams, and concerns.

- Guide him to identify and express his feelings, resist the urge to cut in, or make his ill feelings go away. Wait until he is ready to talk about possible solutions.

Children who know how to express and cope with their changing emotions are more likely to display the following:

- More supportive and empathetic to others
- Perform better in school and career when they mature
- Have better mental health and wellbeing
- Have more stable, loving, and positive relationships
- Feel more confident, competent, and capable
- Display fewer behavioral problems
- Have a positive self-concept
- Develop coping skills and resiliency

Teach your older kid to express his frustration, anger, and other strong emotions by:

- Taking some deep breaths
- Taking time out or walking away
- Taking time to relax, then try again
- Saying what he feels rather than acting it out
- Finding another way to do things
- Asking for support or assistance
- Trying to solve problems with words
- Spending time with you or asking for a cuddle/hug

2. Talk About Your Feelings and Needs

"I Am Sad That You and Your Brother Quarreled."

By telling your child what you feel, you are sending him a message that you do not like him and his sibling quarreling over a toy. And you also expect him to be more tolerant and generous because he is the older one.

It is okay to express your feelings and needs in a way that is clear and does not shame your kid. If you are angry, it is much better to wait until you regain your self-control and talk to him later. Never discipline or problem-solve when you are angry. As a parent, you are the model of the behaviors you want him to acquire. How you respond and handle the conflict impacts the way he responds.

Parenting is a difficult job, which sometimes brings out natural reactions. But remember, that just like your child, you are human and prone to stress, anxiety, and other negative emotions. If you are unhappy, stressed, or worried, it is extremely hard to be objective or handle the situations that involve your child. So, do not underestimate the importance of keeping yourself healthy and in top condition. It is important to take care of your well-being while taking care of your family. Have realistic expectations—for yourself, kids, and spouse. You are not superhuman, and you don't have all the answers. If you need help, talk to your family, friends, and other support systems.

Your child will also appreciate you being open to him, in terms of your own feelings and needs. Share your own childhood experiences and lessons learned. Sharing personal stories will help him see you in a better light, that once upon a time, you were a child like him. Use the opportunity to let him know you better, not just as a mom or dad, but someone who has gone through different experiences.

3. Brainstorm Together and Find a Mutually Agreeable Solution to the Conflict

Sit down and discuss the problem with your child when both of you have calmed down. You can use these simple steps:

1. **Show empathy and concern.** Using a non-accusing, gentle tone, acknowledge your concern for what happened. Avoid making a long lecture. Simply state what you see or observe.

"It Looks Like You and Your Brother Want the Same Ball, But It Is Not Good to Fight."

2. **Define the problem.** Briefly explain why quarreling is not good, especially between siblings. Give emphasis on why it should not happen again and why it is important to change the behavior. Use the "When and then" approach to emphasize the impact of the misbehavior. "When you hit your brother or other people, he feels hurt and sad. Do you want that to happen?"

3. **Ask for ideas.** "What will you do about it?" or "Let's think about ways to prevent it."

4. **Record all the ideas, without evaluating.** Get a pen and paper, then write down all the solutions that you both think of. Listen to his ideas and practical solutions.

5. **Decide and agree on a mutually-acceptable, feasible solution.** Categorize all the answers into

three sections—ideas you both like, don't like, and plan to follow through. Then, review the best suggestions and decide together.

CHAPTER 3:

Using Encouragement Effectively

Encouragement, when used properly, bring positive effects, but indiscriminate or overusing it brings the opposite and do more harm to the kid instead of good.

Encouragement vs. Praise

Encouragement points out specific facts without evaluating them. It is non-judgmental. Examples are "I know that you work hard to finish your project" or "Look at those pretty details in your painting." These examples point out certain things that were highlighted in his performance, but you did not evaluate them. The encouraging words you say develop a sense of pride and enhance his motivation to do better the next time around.

Praise focuses on what parents (adults) feel or think. It often uses judgment like good, nice, best, and so on. For example, "You are such a nice boy." "I like that you are a very good dancer." Sometimes, kids who receive a lot of praise do things to please adults and not because they want to do them.

Yes, it is necessary for children to receive praise or reinforcement, but encouragement is far more powerful when you are disciplining your child, helping him build his self-concept, teaching him values, and motivating him to cooperate. So, when you are about to say "You're a great boy!", change it to "You share your toys with your playmate. Thank you for being generous." This will encourage him to be more generous, compassionate, and proud of his accomplishments.

Other Benefits That Encouragement Brings

- It increases the intrinsic motivation
- It enhances perseverance
- It improves self-esteem and self-confidence
- It sets up children for future success

The key to using encouragement effectively is knowing **when** and **how** to express it.

1. Be Sincere and Honest. Say encouraging words that are consistent with the facts.

Say—"Well done! You did well in your test. Keep up the good work!"

Don't use overly effusive or general words like "You're a genius, I am sure that you will do great again next time!"

2. Be Descriptive and Specific. Refrain from using sweeping statements or comments, which can be perceived as not factually correct. The better way is to point out a specific behavior or skill that helps him perform well. It shows that you really paid attention to his performance and you really care.

Say—"You picked up the right colors for your painting project."

Don't say—"Good job on that one!" or "That was awesome!"

3. Focus On the Effort and the Process, Rather Than Ability. When you attribute your child's achievement to the effort he exerted, he will be motivated to improve his skills through practice. It leads to a growth mindset that increases his persistence, motivation, and enjoyment to master his craft.

On the other hand, a child who is praised for his ability instead of his efforts will also be motivated to try harder and succeed. However, most often than not, children in the praised domain quit faster when they face failure. They suffer from an achievement-based concept that makes them more vulnerable.

Say—"Your strategy was excellent!"

Don't say—"Your ability to solve the problem is excellent!"

4. Avoid Comparison. A comparison can be double-edged. It can be motivating or can be depressing for children, leaving them vulnerable to setbacks.

Say—"Your great focus helped you solve the problem."

Don't say—"You are smarter than your brother."

5. Avoid Handing Out Too Many Encouraging Words for Easy Tasks. It may lead children to avoid complex tasks, and select those that are easy to complete. It also implies that there is originally a lower expectation of competence and parents are over-handing words as an extrinsic reward which lessens, not increases motivation. When it is not given, kids may think that the absence of praise signifies failure. Furthermore, giving it indiscriminately may lead to an over-inflated self-image that develops narcissistic children or constant pressure to outperform the previous performance.

It may give an idea that he is valued because he met the standards, but what if he fails? Does it mean that he is a failure?

Other Motivating Ways to Encourage Your Kid

- **Have fun together**. Allow the child to select a task and do it together, like washing the car or cleaning the yard. The goal is to have fun.

- **Have a regular conversation**. Talking about various topics that interest you and your child is another meaningful activity. The goal is to understand each other better.

- **Listen to your child**. Be willing to listen when he calls your attention. It makes him feel important and subsequently, learn to express his feelings with clarity. The goal is to help your child become more confident and open to share his experiences.

- **Show your love, no matter what**. The most valuable words that your child wants to hear during his down moments like failing to get high grades or make it to the sports team is "I love you." Appreciating his efforts at the moment of sadness is also vital because it will encourage him to do better the next time. The goal is to show that no matter what happens, you are there to support and love him.

- **Admit when you are mistaken and say sorry.** When you are wrong, it's okay to apologize to your child. It conveys that they are not perfect and commit mistakes sometimes. The goal is to teach your child to become responsible for his thoughts and actions and learn to apologize when he is wrong.

- **Exhibit his achievements prominently.** Displaying his trophies, medals, and other proofs of achievement at home encourage the child to accomplish more and be more hardworking. This will make him more receptive to try new things and accept new challenges. The goal is to make him see you proud even without saying them aloud all the time.

- **Create a nostalgic activity.** One fun way is to review his previous years of accomplishments like certificates, art and crafts, projects, pictures, and stories together. Talk about his happy experiences during those winning moments. The goal is to encourage and motivate him to keep doing better.

- **Provide responsibility.** Allow your child to do simple household chores like preparing his favorite meal, picking up trash, or feeding the pets. The goal is to make him feel more capable, responsible, and in control of his world, encouraging him to aspire for bigger things in life.

- **Let him know that he did a good job.** Let him know that you appreciate his efforts by giving a thumbs up, hugging, or treating him with ice cream. Simple gestures like these are more meaningful compared to lavish praises. The goal is to motivate him to keep up doing his best in everything he pursues.

CHAPTER 4:

Listen

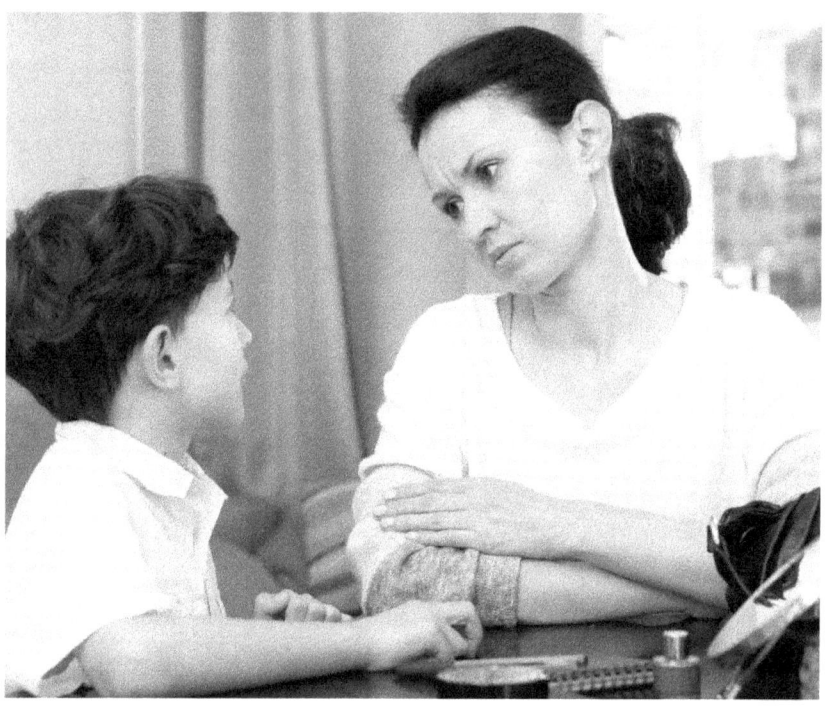

Part of the reason a rich language skillset can be developed has to do with the interaction between the educator/parent and the child.

Getting Down on Their Level, Eye-To-Eye Conversations

Kids of all ages dislike when adults speak to them as if they were less smart or use an authoritative manner. That manner includes tone of voice and body language. Rather than talk to the child at full height, which means you have to look down and look up, why not chat with them on their level, eye to eye. When you do this, the child can better relate to you, and doing so builds trust. It also increases their confidence in their communication skills, encourages them to open up more, and demonstrates the importance of good eye contact. You have an excellent opportunity to put this method into practice when your child is experiencing a tantrum. For instance, rather than scolding them for the outburst, you could make it clear that you acknowledge how they are feeling and that you accept and love them regardless.

For example, you could say something like, "You seem upset/frustrated/hurt/angry. Would you like to show me?" It makes it safe for them to express how they are feeling. When you get into a habit of having eye-to-eye conversations with the child, they will pick up on your "good" practices and do the same when speaking to others. This reflects a child who is equipped with confidence.

Listening and Responding Appropriately

Talk to the child and listen with respect, and you should find they do the same back, as they will unconsciously pick up on your behavior. Here are some useful tips:

- Speak slowly.
- Speak clearly.
- When your child is no longer a baby, try not to speak in "motherese" or using baby talk.
- Bend or crouch down so that you are on the child's level and talk to him or her eye to eye.
- We often expect our child/children to have manners and be courteous, so we must set an example. Say, "please," "thank you," and "may I?"
- Many people have fallen into the bad habit of waiting to speak rather than merely listening to what the other person has to say. When you are listening to your child, allow yourself to be present and look. You may be surprised to find they do the same.
- Although this guide encourages you to use big words (don't be afraid to, it's how they learn), it's okay at times to say very little and allow your child to enjoy being held by you or focus on whatever catches their attention.
- If your child is reacting inappropriately, you can try speaking quietly and lovingly rather than getting angry. They may grow to understand that acting out of fear or with anger isn't necessary.

Asking Questions and Respecting Answers

Often, parents can ask questions that leave the child feeling ashamed or frustrated, and that negativity tends to come from how the question was asked. For example, if the child spills a cup of milk (accidentally or on purpose), your angry or demanding reaction—"Why did you spill your milk??"—can cause the child to react poorly. If you ask the same question in a non-threatening way, you may get a lot further in finding out what's going on with your child. Here are some ways you can ask questions in a way that empowers the child.

1. If you can see that your child is struggling with something, offer to help them. "Would you like any help with putting that back?" "How can I help?" Just give them as much help as they need and then step away.
2. Perhaps you could choose, "Would you like to put on your gloves first or your hat?"
3. Instead of telling your child what to do next, perhaps you could ask them, "What happens next?" This powerful question allows the child to develop independence by getting them accountable for their daily lives.
4. If you are encouraging your child to make something, such as cooking a meal or arts and crafts, it might be useful to help them by asking what they will need. For example, "What materials do we need?"

5. To help your child express their feelings rather than keep them bottled up, you could ask them, "How do you feel about that?"

Positive Language and Positive Discipline Against the Word "No"

First of all, cut yourself some slack if you find yourself saying "no" more often than you would prefer. Avoiding "no" with your child can be difficult, especially if you think it's necessary. Many parents struggle with this word because, like you, they want the best for their children, and sometimes they feel the "best" may involve saying "no," depending on what the situation is. First, understand that infants don't know what the word "no" means. If your child has picked up an inappropriate object, rather than saying "no," take it out of their hands and put it out of reach. Alternatively, you can redirect the child to something else if it seems they are about to grasp something they shouldn't.

You may also find it difficult when a child says "no" to you. Again, there are ways around it. Rather than get cross when your child says "no" to you, change the language. Here are some examples:

You: "It's time for dinner."

Child: "No!"

You: "We are going to eat dinner in five minutes. When you have finished playing that game, let's work together to enjoy a delicious dinner."

Healthy Alternatives and Directed Choice

It's essential to use positive language to help build the child's self-confidence. For example, if you tell a child not to drop the glass, it puts the idea in their head that they could lose it, and then they are more likely to (unconsciously). A mother shared with me an incident when her child was enjoying her time on a swing. When the child called out to her mother and said, "Hey mommy, look at me, this is fun," her mother's face dropped, and she called out with a tone of frustration and concern, "Mind you don't fall off!" The child suddenly picked up on her mother's fear of falling off the swing, which caused her muscles to become weak. Her grip loosened, and guess what? She fell off!

It would be a good idea to reframe our language so that it's more positive and empowering. For instance, rather than say, "Don't drop the glass" or "Don't spill the orange juice," perhaps you could say, "Hold the glass with both hands" or "Stroll while you're carrying that glass."

Sometimes, a situation may involve some physical redirection, not just with what we say but how we respond to situations. For example, if you can see your child is crawling away from you, it may be tempting to scoop them up. However, perhaps you could stand in front of the child to face her/him. This may help redirect the child's movement, so it seems like they are choosing to head in a different direction.

If you redirect your child's behavior every time you feel it's appropriate to do so, it teaches them that there are some limits, but does so lovingly and respectfully.

Emotional Learning

Affirming Your Child's Emotions

It may be challenging in the beginning, but over time you may be pleased with the results. If your child is visibly upset, rather than saying, "stop sulking" or "mind your temper," you could instead say something like, "I see you're feeling angry. Why don't you draw how you're feeling...? Wow, that's a big circle, you must be feeling so angry." (You'll know instinctively what to say, this is simply a guide).

Mindfulness/Breathing Techniques

Mindfulness is extremely powerful for adults, and the power is even higher in children! Too many people today live their daily lives in a state of tension, and often they don't realize it. They are so used to being stressed out that they may believe they're relaxed when they aren't. They may not know how to balance themselves because it generally isn't something people are taught growing up. If you can help your child be mindful, you provide them with an enormous gift that can serve them well into adulthood.

Here are some of the benefits for your child:

- Increased social interaction and confidence when communicating with others
- Better focus on tasks
- Improved resilience
- Decreased stress and anxiety
- Encouragement to adopt a more positive attitude towards life
- Improved and regulated emotions—Children are less likely to react to situations.
- Enhanced self-esteem and confidence
- Better health (physical, mental, and emotional) and well-being

Since kids learn so quickly, they will take in information like a sponge. The process of teaching them mindfulness and breathing techniques doesn't need to be long and complicated. Remember the KISS method! Here are some ways you can start to teach mindfulness and breathing techniques to your children:

- Regularly encourage children to think of five things that make them feel happy, that make them smile, or they feel grateful for.
- Get them to breathe in and squeeze all of their muscles so that they have tensed up for a few moments and then let go, taking a deep breath out. This exercise helps to relax the body and breathe out any tension. Lead by example and do the workout with them (it will calm you too).

- Ask your child to put one or both hands on their heart and feel the heartbeat while taking deep breaths; through the nose, hold the breath for three seconds, and then slowly exhale through the mouth.
- Walk with your child in nature. Get them to engage their five senses by observing the environment and reporting what they see, hear, feel, and taste. Ask them what textures they think of when they pick up items or touches tree trunks.
- Meditate with your child. Although you will both be silent, it's still a great way to increase the bond between you.
- Whenever your child seems stressed out, tell them to "stop." Then suggest that they take a few deep breaths and start to observe how they are feeling, what they are thinking, and ask them to breathe out the stress.
- Have positive uplifting words displayed somewhere in the child's bedroom. That way, upon waking up in the mornings and going to bed at night, your child will see these words of encouragement.
- Where possible, have children take off their shoes and socks. Suggest that they walk around barefoot in the garden while they take deep breaths and observe. This will help them to stay grounded.

CHAPTER 5:

Pay Attention

When your Child Needs Special help

There are certain situations in life when you need to pay special attention to your kid. It is not necessary that your kid needs special attention only when he is with some special needs. A normal kid in his life needs some special attention in order to meet up the regular challenges. The core concept to understand is the need for such help in the normal routine as well. Not all the kids are able to do everything at the same pace. At some point in their social and educational life, they need to do things differently. As parents, it is necessary for you to identify when your kid needs special attention and help from you.

Here are some situations when you need to be there with kids.

Unable to Focus

If your kid is unable to focus on anything whether it is a practical demonstration or learning then you should get an idea of something happening wrong. Maybe the kid is not interested in the activity or exposed to some confusions or fears. You can help the kid in understanding the activity and help him to focus on the situation without getting worried about anything else.

Having Sleep Issues

One of the core issues that kids have is at bedtime. Sometimes they are scared of darkness, isolation, or nightmares as well. In such a situation, forcing the kid to sleep is not a good idea. You need to make him deal with the situation and fight back all the ideas and fears in his mind.

Health Is Not On a Good Note

When the kids are not feeling well, they are in a vulnerable situation. They can react to things differently all the time. Mood swings, anger, sadness all of these feelings can come up together or on an interval basis. You need to understand the situation and help your child to overcome the fear or feeling of not being so well at that specific time.

Unable to Express

Some kids are not good with expression. They do not have any idea about the selection of words or expressions to say what they feel. When there is a situation of unrest, you need to help the kid by understanding behaviors. At this time, you can rescue the kid by helping him in feeling comfortable to tell you what is cooking insides his mind.

Mixed Feelings of Anger, Excitement, and Sorrow

One of the critical situations with a child is when he is unable to identify the real feeling. At this time, he behaves differently due to the mixed emotions toward a happening or person. You need to help the kid about knowing what is happening to him and why. Moreover, you should help the kids to deal with such conditions efficiently.

Growing as a Family: Finding Support, Resources, and Sanity

Positive discipline is not about letting your kid learn all the things independently. It is not a kind of high school training where your kid needs to learn everything on his own. It is about a family, a home, and all the peers together. If you want your kids to be healthy in body and mind as well, you need to grow as a family.

Family is not just about having food together, living in a house, going on vacations, and all the good things. Family is there for anyone in the hard times and bad things as well. To encourage positive discipline in your kids it is necessary to make them understand the need and importance of the family. When you are good enough to maintain a good family system, you will be able to make things better.

A person craves three things from his family, support, resources, and sanity. All these three things have integral importance in the overall learning of kids and their growth as well. The most important thing is to consider that without these three elements a family cannot have a healthy future.

Your Support Is the Key

When you are teaching the kids about positive discipline and way of life then you need to provide them complete support.

There can be multiple behaviors on the go that your kid will express in the beginning. You are supposed to understand these actions, reactions and then support the kid accordingly. For his or her good, you need to understand the need and then as a family, you need to support them.

The issue can be anything; it can be a failure, a bad habit, some physical or psychological deficiency, or any health issue as well. In all the phases, the support and shelter by the family in the right manner can help the kid to sustain the situation.

The support to your kid in a critical situation is not that you are covering up the mistakes or giving an exit from something wrong. It is about making the kid understand what's right and what makes things wrong as a whole.

Even if your kid has done something that is not right you need to make him realize the mistake and support him to make a correction. On the other hand, if your kid is unable to learn new things then you need to adopt the things that can help him with a better understanding of the issue. This support of the family will increase your kid's reliance on family and he will look towards the family in any need or situation that demands support.

Hit the Help Resources

Finding the resources to help your kids and family is another important thing that makes a family. If there is something that went wrong, there is a fault line in your kids or a deficiency; you need to hit the right resources to help. These resources can be personal, individual, family-based, and outsourced as well. You need to identify the appropriate resource as per the need.

Medical Attention

Feeling unwell is one of the common problems faced by the kids. Anything new that happens to them makes them feel sick. It is not about the real medical problem all the time but sometimes a change in hormones, conditions, and brain activities. Sometimes, kids can be serious too. Medical changes are a kind of complex issue that can hit the kids badly. In such matters other than family support and condolence, medical attention and professional help are necessary. Make sure to be with your kid all the time as it is necessary for him to have someone he can trust and really on. It can help the kid not to panic.

Additional Attention

Sometimes, kids need additional or special attention when going through a feeling or phase. Mostly, it happens in case of any loss, trauma, or bad health. You need to use your attention as a resource and give the maximum attention and time to the kid. It will help him to get close to you and open to the issues and problems. The close relation can help to make things even better between the families and keep the unit connected.

Discussion and Debate

Sometimes the perceptions about the problem are not good enough. You need to discuss and debate the issue with the kids. At this moment, the kids can express what they actually feel and what are the real problems they have regarding a specific issue. This can actually help in making a real difference in the overall situation. As a family, it is important to discuss issues, conflicts, and problems with each other in a healthy environment.

Educational Grooming

Sometimes there are behavioral issues that kids have shown in certain situations. It is because they do not have any education about dealing with the situations. You need to invest time and look into the educational grooming of the child. It is about solving the problem he is having inside his mind and make things even for the rest.

Getting Study Kits

If the child is unable to study well, then you can get him the study kits. These resources help a child to know things better. Using simple and easy themes, these kits can breakdown the complex terms easily and let the kid know better and more. You need to select these kits carefully in order to get the right results.

Understand the Variation

It is not necessary that all the kids are of the same nature and have the same needs, behaviors, and reactions to things. If your kid is behaving differently than others it is necessary for you to know that everyone is different from each other. This variation is the beauty of humankind. This difference makes a person capable of doing something different from the other do. To grow as a family, you need to understand this concept of variation and take further steps for improvement.

Explore the Options

Other than support, resources, and understanding there are multiple options you have to make your family stronger and kids table. Remember, it is not necessary that if you have a challenging kid only then you need to pay extra attention. For every kid, there is a need to look around for the best options and get the right things in the box. Every single kid is different and you need to explore the options for all your kids differently. You cannot match all your three kids—if there are—with each other and expect them to behave the same way.

Here are some other practical things that you are supposed to consider and work on:

Match Interests

Being a parent, you need to be the closest friends to your kids. It is only possible when you are sharing the same interests with them. It is not possible that the whole family will have the same interests but they can grow. As parents, you can set up some of the common habits for all the kids so everyone can have a good time together. On the other hand, do not restrict any new interests of your kids. In fact, you can participate in the other activities with them so they can rely on you. It will help your kids to share what they feel and how they perceive the other things around them. Moreover, you can help them grow better by knowing things better.

Participate to Make It Rational

If your kids are differently doing something because they are unable to do it the way others do then it's fine. You do not have to be worried, instead of getting them out of their comfort zone you are supposed to make their zone comfort for themselves. As far as your kid is trying hard to be something, so you are supposed to help with that. Your participation in the task can make this unique style rational and it will not make your kid feel awkward about it. Something with participation you can make your kid learn the right or rational way to do something. All you need is to observe, participate, and anticipate the problem.

Boost Your Kid's Confidence

If your kid is doing something different that is not as per the specific gender or social roles for him, you are supposed to support him in every manner. It is important to boost his confidence with the best arguments and tools. You can make the kid feel normal about his diversity and do not make him answerable for the diversity in him. The actions of support can help him to be better with everything exclusive he holds in himself.

CHAPTER 6:

The Listening Process

To understand your listening behavior, and to increase your active listening skills, you are going to learn about the listening process. Don't be afraid! A little theory will help you to understand listening, and give you the knowledge to apply it to your interactions.

There are several stages involved in the process of listening. Despite being distinct phases, they happen almost simultaneously as you look. They are, in brief, as follows:

Receiving—This is the physical function of hearing, where you receive the actual sound as vibrations in your ear, and transmitted to your brain. As well as audio, any visual cues such as body language and eye contact will also be picked up.

Attending—When the message has been received, i.e. physically picked up on by your senses and carried to your brain, it must then participate. At this stage, it is your job to pay attention to the message by holding it firmly in the short term memory (Baddley & Hitch, 1974). The more attention you pay to the signals of the speaker at this stage, the more likely you are of taking in what is communicated. It is essential in active listening to pay close attention to the speaker because without doing so, and it is impossible to interpret and respond to what is said.

Perceiving—as the amount of attention you pay to the speaker, your perceptions are also a part of the listening process. This may sound unusual at first, but your background, experiences, beliefs, and your state of mind at the time, will all affect the message that you eventually receive. In short, you hear what you want to hear, or sometimes what you expect to hear. This is one of the reasons why two people may listen to a different message from the same speaker; their perceptual filters have screened out or amplified different parts of the word.

You must have a perceptual filter. There are so many potential incoming signals in the world that it would simply blow your mind to take them all in. This can even be seen in essential functions like crossing the road, where you will notice (if you try to notice) that you will be more attuned to the noise of cars, speed, and distance, and to move in that moment. You may also blank out a lot of what else is around until you have made it to the other side.

Interpreting—So far on the journey, you have picked up the speaker's communication with your senses, which have carried it to the brain. You have held your attention on it for long enough that you have remembered it, and your perceptions have meanwhile done a great job of filtering out what is not needed, or what is in too severe a conflict with your conceptual outlook. Now, communication will be processed for meaning.

Your brain does this by attempting to fit the message into the correct linguistic categories, where it can discern for meaning according to your previous experiences, thoughts and beliefs, and long term memory. Linguistic groups are a technical term for how we break down layman's for the sake of categorizing it, and if needed analyzing it.

In layman's terms, this means that you interpret, and possibly an analysis of what has been said. You speaker's yourself at this point what understanding you can take from the speaker's message, and what the meaning is. Often the original meaning can be distorted, and can even end up completely different from what meant initially been.

One of the main aims of active listening is that it aims to understand what was meant by the speaker, rather than assuming our interpretation is correct.

Responding—The final stage of the listening process is the response. Internally, you are moving the message from short term to long term memory, in case you need to retrieve it at a later point. The external response is given in the form of feedback, which may be an agreement, a reiteration or paraphrase, or a question regarding the message. The answer is an essential part of listening. Research by Leavitt and Mueller (1968) showed that the listener and speaker both gain confidence that the message has been understood and both experience a high degree of satisfaction in conversation when feedback is given. This is something that active listening places a lot of emphasis on, and will be covered in more detail later on in the book. A response can go beyond feedback and can represent a transition between listening and speaking.

Chinese Whispers

You may be a little bogged down after that, but you must be familiar with the listening process; it provides a solid foundation for everything that is to come. For now, you can consider the above method of listening in the context of a game of Chinese whispers.

If you are not familiar with the game, Chinese whispers played in a group, who sit in a circle. Someone picked to start the game, by coming up with a message to pass on to the person next to them. They think of a word and whisper it in the next person's ear, and it's passed all the way around. The last person in the circle shouts the message out loud, and the original speaker reveals the original message. Then everyone laughs at how much the world has changed, and tries to work out where the distortions occurred.

So, where do the distortions occur? How does "My uncle packed sandwiches for all of us to take to the beach," become "Try walking up this way to get to get to the sweets."?

Well, the distortions could occur at any point during the communication, and the more people the message goes around, the more distorted it is likely to become.

It could be a lack of attention and only part of the message received by someone. It could be that the message has been screened out by bias, or misinterpreted by the impressions of someone. If the idea is emotionally charged or opinionated, then this is even more likely.

If you have not played this game yet, then consider getting it together to see how flawed our listening can be, even when the message is simple.

Why Is It Helpful to Understand This Process?

It is easy to see from studying the listening process described above that listening is a somewhat complicated process involving multiple aspects. Instead of merely labeling yourself as a "bad listener," you can begin to understand what you can improve upon, or what stage of the listening process might be causing you to miss what is going on in the communication.

Do you pay enough attention to what is said? Is there a reason for you not doing it? Are there too many actions in the room? Maybe you block out the real message because you don't want to hear it; it could be your perceptual filter that causes you to cross wires with your loved ones. You could be misinterpreting the message that your friend is expressing. You may not be providing enough feedback for the speaker, who is relying on your response to engage in the conversation.

By understanding the whole process of listening, you can begin to see it differently. You can start to understand it.

A Positive Listening Attitude

Just in case your mind has been blown by the theory covered so far, you will be glad to know the tension is going to be momentarily released, and some simple advice offered to all of you. All of the steps of the process above can easily enhance with a positive listening attitude.

A positive listening attitude is to be interested in what is said. It varies across the conversation, and natural interest rises and falls depending on your concern for the message at hand. But being genuinely interested in what people have to say, and being open-minded towards new perspectives, helps you to function smoothly as a listener. Where your loved ones are concerned, you should always be interested.

Seeing listening as an active role in interaction also helps to cultivate this attitude. As a listener, it is your job to facilitate conversation. Please begin to see listening for the shining grace that it is; it is a valuable skill, and it helps people to feel relaxed in their relationships with you.

Start to enjoy listening; be positive open-minded.

What Is an Active Listener?

You may have seen the words "active listener" mentioned several times in this book already; you may have also seen it mentioned elsewhere.

In Western culture, we often listen in a somewhat passive way; we wait our turn while the other person speaks. We keep quiet out of respect for their message. Often, we are waiting for our turn again.

The active listener is engaged. They are as much a part of the conversation as the speaker because they see themselves as being partially responsible for the communication. They have a positive attitude towards listening; they are consciously working out what the message means, what angle the speaker is approaching from, and what their response may be. An active listener gives full attention to the conversation and is interested in what is said, why it is said, and how the speaker can be encouraged.

CHAPTER 7:

Act Without Words: The Secret of Staying Calm

When your toddler is full-swing into a tantrum, you may find that you are entirely desperate to get it to stop as soon as possible. You may think that you can get your child to stop if you give in, or if you simply put your child in a time out, you can get rid of the whole problem. You may attempt to do just about anything that comes to mind in hopes of stopping that tantrum before it can blow up. Many people think that stopping a tantrum is next to impossible or that their children are simply acting difficult on purpose, but you can actually help your child to recognize what is happening, why the behavior is a problem in the first place, and how to eliminate the behavior altogether. The trick to this is quite simple—all you need to do is use breathing.

Think about it—when you are highly emotional, what do you do to help yourself calm down, regain control, and get back on track? Most people use deep breathing activities. This makes sense biologically—when you take in a big, deep breath, you change the pressure within your chest. This then results in your heart rate having to fluctuate to accommodate, which happens due to the vagus nerve activating. The vagus nerve, which regulates your heart and your circulatory system, is also responsible for relaxation and calming down, and when you take big, deep breaths, you encourage your body to relax as well. You get yourself to stop and relax when you use those big, deep breaths for yourself and in doing so, you help yourself relax.

Even young children can learn how to do this as well. You may not be able to tell them to take a big breath, but you can guide them using different methods as well. You can essentially encourage your child to take big, deep breaths through playing with them, and when they do so, they begin to calm down. This can be encouraged and you can tell your child about how it helps them calm down with ease. When you do this, you are going to find that you can help them calm down.

Over time, your children learn how to figure out how to calm themselves down as well. They learn to self-regulate because they start to associate the deep breathing exercises with ways that they can calm down. They do this to self-soothe, and this can help them learn to prevent themselves from throwing a tantrum as well. They will learn exactly how they can defeat those tantrums themselves, allowing them to be able to self-regulate.

Let's really quickly take a look at three different ways that you can trigger your child to breathe slowly and deeply in order to get them to calm down. Keep in mind that if you want these exercises to be effective in the long run, you will always want to encourage them to begin with your child in a calmer state. This allows for all sorts of practice so your child knows what to expect. When you do this on a regular basis, you will find that your child will be able to access these exercises with ease when they really matter.

- Flowers and candles: One method that children love to use when they need to breathe is through the use of visualization and pretend. You can do this by encouraging your child to sniff a flower and then blow out a candle that you pretend to hold. When you do this, you encourage your child to stop and breathe, allowing them to really start to calm down. For the greatest impact, guide them into sniffing the flower of whatever scent you know your child likes, and then tell your child to blow out a big birthday cake candle that you are holding. You are then encouraging a big, deep sniff and a big, deep blow.

- Belly breathing: This method is also going to work the same way—you are encouraging your child to breathe through his or her stomach instead of with the chest, which some people can find that they do when they are stressed out. All you will do is have your child lay down on his or her back and place a stuffed animal or a rock on their stomachs. Then, encourage them to breathe deeply to watch the stuffed animal move up and down as they do. This does not only helps your child breathe; it encourages your child to be distracted. Your child is now more interested in the toy and has breathed deeply to calm down.

- Playing with feathers: You can use feathers that you have found poking out of down pillows and jackets, or you can buy craft feathers at the store. When you do this, you can encourage your child to blow feathers up into the air. They will toss the feather into the air and then blow at it to move it around. Once again, you get the double benefit of encouraging all sorts of big, deep breaths while also ensuring that your child is being distracted by something fun. You can even take this a step further with many different in different shapes and sizes—you and your child can make it a game to see which ones will go further than the others.

- Dragon breaths: Another way that you can make sure that your child is going to breathe deeply is by encouraging your child to breathe out their anger. If your child is feeling angry or frustrated, you can have them take in a big, deep breath, lift up their heads to look at the sky, and then breathe out as hard as they can. Tell them to breathe out their anger when you do this, like a dragon breathing fire.

Mindful Hugging

Sometimes, your child needs attention. This is normal—they require that connection with their parents to be able to survive and that means that they need to get it from somewhere. One of the best ways that you can do so is through hugging, cuddling, and generally being affectionate with them. When your child is stuck in a tantrum, you may find that he or she is going to be best served by debating giving your child that connection with someone else. You may need to try to calm them down through hugs and cuddles, while still recognizing body autonomy where you can.

When your child is calm, you can make sure that you give your child a mindful hug—doing this will ensure that your child is getting all of that affection and care that she needs when she needs it rather than waiting for your child to get so upset that he or she feels the need to act out to get it. When you do this, acting in ways that are mindful with hugs, you can encourage and facilitate that bonding with your child in a way that is going to help mitigate those future tantrums. You will be ensuring that you can, in fact, get around the feelings of resentment that the child may otherwise begin to develop if you do not give her the affection needed when it is needed in the first place.

When you hug your child, you trigger the production of oxytocin in both you and your child. In doing so, stress hormones begin to drop. You calm your child naturally when you do this and that is a very powerful thing. When you can facilitate this on a regular basis, you will find that your child is much more capable of self-regulating. Your child will feel better just due to the lessened stress hormones. Your child will feel more agreeable because they will know that they can trust that they can get those cuddles in when they matter the most.

Further, when you do establish this sort of hugging, you will be able to ask your child mid-tantrum if they need a hug. If they know that hugs feel good and make them feel better, they will know that they can count on you to help them feel better in the first place. They will be much more willing to acknowledge mid-tantrum that what they really need is a big, mindful hug when you have taught them to do exactly that to help them cope with the world around them. When you use this method with your child, you will find that they will have fewer tantrums and that the tantrums that they do have will be easier to tame.

When you want to involve mindful hugging, you are looking for hugs that are going to involve you entirely focusing on that hug for the moment that you are in it. You will want to take your child in your arms for longer than just a split second and allow them to feel you and really relate to you at that moment. It is very powerful—it lights up the areas in your brain that are responsible for rewarding you.

Hugging should be something that you engage in regularly. It should never be used as a way for you to try to punish your child—you should not intentionally withhold your affection if your child comes looking for it. Rather, you should always try to accommodate it. One way that you can do so is to encourage a mindful hug once a day, in which you and your child will hug each other tightly and closely for at least three big, slow, deep breaths. You should try to synchronize your own breathing to that of your child's so you can really relate at that moment. When you do this, you ensure that you feel how close you are to your child and your child will feel that closeness with you as well. Your child will begin to relax in your arms and you will feel closer and better with them.

You can take this a step further if your toddler is quite verbal—you can ask how that hug makes them feel and ask whether they seem to like it. When you do ask your toddler about their own feelings, consider how it is that your child seems to be feeling as a result. You may find that your child is quite happy to have hugged you and will go out of their way to seek it even more than before. When you are hugging your child, try to keep the following tips in mind:

- Hug with your whole body and awareness—you should focus entirely on your child when you do this. Try to feel the weight of your child in your arms and how it makes you feel

- Hug regularly every morning and before bed, and also any time you and your child part

- Make sure that you put away any distractions when you do hug your child and ensure that you are really present when you do so

- Always offer a hug when you see that your child is getting overwhelmed or frustrated to help defuse the situation

CHAPTER 8:

Bad Words

They pop out of your child's mouth at what seems like the worst moments. He or she seems to be announcing to the world that you are a terrible parent and that you have exposed him or her to terrible things. They are going to let everyone know that they heard those words, even if they have no idea what they mean.

It can be a complete shock the first time that your child drops a putty mouth bomb, especially when it is in front of friends or family. We spend so many years, trying to help them build their vocabularies, understand what words mean, and watch every word we say in front of them when all of a sudden, this filthy word pours out of your baby's mouth as if he or she has been hearing it since birth.

The first thing that you need to understand is that no, toddlers have no idea what these words mean, they only understand that somewhere they heard someone use one, and it was used in an emotionally charged situation.

Toddlers will pick up on these words very quickly. Often, it only takes them hearing it one time for it to stick in their little heads and pop out of their mouths when you least expect it to.

There is no way, no matter how hard you try or how protective a parent you are that you can protect them from learning these words. It does not matter that you do not use them in your home, chances are that the child is exposed to someone that does use these words or they are exposed to the child of someone that does use these words. They can hear them on television, remember, they may not always be completely asleep as you are watching your favorite television shows in the evening. They can hear them slip out of your mouth as you are cut off in traffic, or they can learn them from the kids in daycare. No matter what, these words are always there and just because they pop out of your toddler's mouth, it does not mean you are a bad parent.

Your child is simply mimicking what he or she heard someone else say, and they are trying to find out what happens when they say it. One huge mistake that I see parents do is that they burst out laughing, whether it be from embarrassment or whether they actually think that it is funny when their child blurts out a bad word. This is a huge mistake because it is teaching the child that you think what they did is funny; it is encouraging them to do it in the future and not teaching them that they should not talk like this.

One thing that taught me very early on not to use these types of words especially in front of my children was that studies showed those who used curse words were of lower intelligence than those that did not. I never wanted to be the type of person that came across as lacking intelligence, so I did my best to ensure these words did not come out of my mouth.

I am sure that you do not want yourself nor your child to give the appearance of lacking intelligence so when these words come out of the child's mouth, it is important that you do not laugh or make jokes about it but instead, show the child that it is a serious matter.

Curse words are not the only nasty language that comes out of a toddler's mouth. Toddlers often begin using potty language, well, when they start potty training.

We have to remember that toddlers can be rude, they can be mean and, even though they do not mean to be, it is simply not acceptable behavior. We have to nip it in the bud before it gets worse.

When you begin potty training, it is important that you teach the child that words such as poop need to remain in the bathroom. You do not want to suffer the embarrassment when your child announces to the cashier at the grocery store that she smells like poop simply because he or she knows that word will get a reaction out of you.

That is one of the main reasons that children use potty language; they know that this type of language is going to get some reaction out of you, and they are using it as a means of controlling the way that you react. This also happens when a toddler begins using swear words and sees that they can get a huge reaction out of you.

The best way to stop this type of behavior is to start at home. When you hear the child say a potty word, you need to let the child know that this is not how we talk, that the specific word is either not allowed or that it is used to define a specific bodily function and nothing more. Do not react as if the world is going to end because your child said a word that they may not really understand. This will only encourage them to continue speaking this way in the future. Instead, remain calm and explain to the child that they are not allowed to speak that way and that it is not polite.

You have to keep a poker face on when your child says a swear word or a potty word. When a child learns that they can make an adult laugh, angry or upset, they are going to continue to display the behavior simply because they saw that it got a reaction out of those around him or her.

Even if the child invents a new word, and you think it is just adorable or funny such as "poopy face snot breath," do not laugh. Do not smile, and do not encourage that type of talk. Let the child know that it is not acceptable and that they should not speak that way. Use a low tone of voice, showing the child that you are disappointed in the way that they were speaking. The child is going to understand quickly that you do not approve, and even if he or she was trying to be funny, chances are it is not going to happen again anytime soon.

It is also important for the child to know words that will allow him or her to express themselves without using curse words or potty language. For example, if you notice that your child is using potty words to express his or her anger, teach the child how to say, "I'm mad."

Never take the time to explain what swear words mean to a toddler. The toddler does not need to know. Instead, if the toddler is stuck on a swear word, and no matter what you do will not give up the word, you are going to have to get a bit stricter and start doling out discipline when the word is used.

Since the child does not quite understand what empathy is yet, it is going to be hard for them to understand how a simple word can upset someone. However, it is important for you to explain this to them, especially if the word that they are saying could be construed as racist or derogatory. Again, you do not have to tell the child what the word means, but let the child know that the word causes hurt feelings and is not nice to say.

Above all, it is important that you watch what is coming out of your mouth. How do you ever expect your child to understand that it is not okay to say bad words when that's all they hear coming out of your mouth?

Take the time to expand your vocabulary, find a different way to vent your anger, whether it be through exercise or even writing in a journal. Once you stop saying these words, you will be amazed at how simple-minded other people sound to you when they are spewing them out of their mouths.

There is no bigger step that you can take which will ensure that your children are not using curse words like this one.

It is also important that you pay attention to the language that other adults use around your children. Of course, there are going to be those rude, obnoxious people in the store or out in public that feel everyone around them needs to hear their filthy mouth. If this is you, STOP. No one wants to hear these words come out of your mouth!

When this happens, as a parent, it is difficult for us not to say anything. However, instead of getting into an argument with someone about the way that they are talking in a public area, just let your child know in a quiet voice that this is not how we talk and that those words should not have been said.

What about when it is someone that your child spends a lot of time with? This can get a little tricky, but one thing that we make sure that all of our guests know is that swearing is not allowed in our homes. It is not just a rule that the children live by, but it is a rule that everyone who walks in our door must follow as long as they are in our home.

This leads to the question: What if we are in someone else's home or on an outing with a friend? Most people will be respectful if you simply tell them that you would appreciate it if they watched what they said when they were around you and your child.

Everyone that knows me knows that they will not hear a curse word come out of my mouth, for that reason, they are very careful when they speak in my presence because they know that I personally find these words offensive. This also means that they are very careful about what they say when they are around my children.

When your child sees this, the child will understand that the person is being respectful of you, and that is the last thing I want to talk about; you need to teach your child to be respectful. Not just when it comes to the words that come out of their mouth but in all of their daily life.

The way that this is done is to be the example that you want your children to follow. Lead them by example teaching them how to treat people and not to gossip about people behind their backs, how to be kind, and share with those that need our help.

I will never forget the day when my daughter was in Head Start. She was about three years old, and there was a project about moms. Her job was to write down why her mom was special. She wrote: My mom is special because she feeds the stray cats in the neighborhood, and she cooks for my neighbors when they are sick.

Never in my life had I known more than I knew at that moment that I was doing the right thing and teaching my child how to respect not only people but the entire world around her. She saw the example I was setting, and she was proud of it. That was the type of person that she wanted to be.

CHAPTER 9:

Handling Tantrums

Not every toddler has tantrums, but most do. They are most common between ages two and three when there can be as many as one to two days for several weeks, and others intermittently. Not all tantrums were created equal. Telling them apart can be tricky.

Stress Tantrums

The toddler is stressed (tired, hungry, ill, or cranky due to several small disappointments, changes, and defeats) when some unpleasant thing happens. Perhaps he hates to have his diaper changed, and Dad insisted on it. Or Mom kept her hands on the grocery cart when he wanted to push it himself. Or his toy broke. That one small incident becomes the straw that broke the camel's back, and suddenly the toddler loses control. The screaming and carrying-on are out of proportion to the problem because the upset isn't about a single event. It's the result of an accumulation of stress that has taken its toll on a tyke who, because of his age, doesn't have a lot of emotional control, to begin with.

Trying to sidestep a stress tantrum may merely be postponing the inevitable. As things heat up, it becomes increasingly clear that the toddler is trying to provoke a struggle.

To manage stress tantrums:

1. Hold the child firmly but lovingly and provide reassurance that she'll be okay in a bit. This assumes you can hold her. Children may thrash too wildly to be safely stored.
2. If she's endangering himself, other people, or property as she rolls about the floor, clear the area if you can. Otherwise, move her to a safe place, like a carpeted floor.
3. Let her cry it out. Tears are an excellent tension reliever.
4. Empathize with the fact that she's having a hard day.
5. When the tantrum ends, ask if she'd like to sit on your lap, rock her, lie down, and have you rub her back.
6. Provide reassurance that things will get more comfortable for her when her new tooth comes through, she's rested, she's adjusted to her new daycare center, or the stressful situation has passed.

When it comes to stress tantrums, the best cure lies in prevention. Consider them a signal that your toddler is under more pressure than she can manage and see if there's a way to help lessen it. Remember that toddlers are already under a lot of stress because they struggle with their sense of inadequacy from wanting to do things and being unable to do them, having lots to communicate and being unable to say much, and wanting to be independent while being emotionally needy.

In a stress tantrum, the child isn't trying to get something; instead, she tries to get rid of the unpleasant feelings that have accumulated. Having a momentary whim gratified helps a stressed toddler feel better, but not for long. The next small crisis produces another upset of similar or even greater intensity because the real problem—feeling generally overwhelmed—remains.

Manipulative Tantrums

Once their end is achieved—freedom to run around the store, liberation from the car seat, permission to eat the cookie, or a toy—they settle down. Tantrums in public are common because many children have learned if they stage a big one, they will immediately be taken home, which is what they want. But of course, every time you appease the child by giving in, you drive home the lesson that screaming, hitting, kicking, thrashing, breath-holding, fainting, and even head-banging and vomiting are workable ways to achieve goals. If the behaviors during manipulative tantrums are particularly dramatic, discuss the problem with your pediatrician to satisfy yourself that—ignoring it—is a safe option. Actions that warrant a professional opinion include banging his head or other self-injurious behavior, passing out, precipitating an asthma attack, or vomiting.

To end manipulative tantrums:

- If she's a raging puddle on the floor, tell her you'll talk to her when she's settled down.
- Carry her to an open space where she can't harm herself or something else, preferably with carpet to soften the blows, if she's flinging herself around.
- Step over her and busy yourself nearby (but out of kicking range) by studiously ignoring her.
- Remain alert to what is happening so you can intervene if she tries to hurt herself or something else.

The challenge is not to take manipulative tantrums personally. See them for what they are: a child's rage at rules and limits. By failing to give in and not paying attention to her, you're showing what happens when people are assailed by crushing disappointments: life goes on. When a tantrum ends, and the child has settled down:

- See it as the victory it is—the child regained control on her own.
- Don't attempt to discuss what transpired before or during the tantrum—let the subject drop.
- Be warm enough to show her you're not angry with her—respond to her desire to be held, hear a story, or participate in another quiet activity once she's settled down.
- Don't try to compensate for having held firm by being overly solicitous.

If throwing a tantrum has worked in the past, the predictable short-term result when parents don't give in is an increase in both the intensity and frequency of tantrums. Confused youngsters work harder to employ the strategy that has worked so well in the past to get their way. It may take several scenes before they grasp that tantrums are no longer a useful method for getting what they want.

Communication Tantrums

Sometimes toddlers throw tantrums out of sheer frustration over their inability to communicate their needs. For instance, your toddler wants something. It's clear to your toddler that you have it. Try as you might, you can't figure out what your child is asking. Get the message across, and then dissolves.

Or it is all too clear what your toddler wants: ice cream. He is sure it is in the freezer because that's where it's kept. Except that there isn't any ice cream there or anywhere else because you're fresh out. He's sure you're withholding it, and you can't find a way to explain it to him. Maybe she wants to watch a particular video, but the tape is broken. Or he wants his pacifier, but it's lost. The only recourse is to provide reassurance that you would give him what he wanted if you could and let him rage at the injustice of it.

It's not easy being of any age, but it can be incredibly hard to be a toddler. Parents who remain sympathetic as children struggle through these trying moments may also feel helpless. Remember that by demonstrating your love for your youngster when she is at her very worst, you are helping a lot.

What to Do During Tantrums

There are many ideas about the best way to intervene during a tantrum. I am going to quickly spell out some general truths about tantrum intervention.

There are a lot of exercises in this book, divided according to the age of your child, to help you create meaningful interventions that work for you. But for now, here are a few quick and easy rules that always apply:

- Stay calm. The key to all successful parenting—and most certainly to effective intervention during tantrums—is parental **self-control**. We will review some more practical steps to make it easier for you to keep your cool in the exercises following "part 2."

- Ask yourself why. Considering the motivation for the behavior can be very helpful. It might be helpful to reframe the question as "What is my child struggling with?"

- Empathize with the child's feelings. The feelings are never the problem; it is what the child is doing with those feelings that can become problematic. Acknowledging the feelings, without judgment, is a great first step.

- Ignore the behavior, not the child. A lot of times, it is very effective to ignore the tantrum. The trick is to first communicate that you are available, loving, and patient but that you're not going to participate in the tantrum. The connection is the key. "I can see that you're very angry. I am sorry. I am going to make dinner now, and I hope that you will help me once you have calmed down."

- Be consistent. Many parents create rules on the fly and react quickly when things go wrong, which leaves little room for forethought and makes consistency very hard. The goal, however, is to try to make similar choices in similar situations and to hold relatively consistent boundaries. Trust that creating space for planning and forethought is a priority because consistency is a very helpful intervention (and prevention) for tantrums.

- Offer alternatives. If your toddler's goals are acceptable, help them find more appropriate means to achieve them. If your child is full of energy and won't stop running in the house, let them run outside with your supervision. If they are angry and throwing things, help them find safer ways to express the anger in their bodies, like stomping their feet or throwing pillows. There are healthy, non-hurtful ways to express emotions.

CHAPTER 10:

How to Replace Punishment with Positive Parenting

A positive approach to parenthood implies an understanding of the child and of his or her behavior, paying attention to how the child feels. What does that mean practically? Seeing what is behind a child's behavior means seeing the real cause, understanding it, and offering the child an alternate solution to negative behavior.

Adults mostly only see the "final product"—the unwanted behavior that they want to correct, or a symptom of the real cause. If they want the child to learn something and that isn't working, it is up to adults to explain to the child the consequences of his negative behavior: natural consequences ("You are cold because you do not want to wear a sweater.") and logical consequences ("We are late for the birthday party because you wanted to play even though the clock was ringing and telling us it was time to go.").

Positive parenting requires a calm tone of voice with a previous agreement and an explanation of what is acceptable and what is not, as well as what will happen if the child does not adhere to the agreement. Positive parenting creates a space for learning without guilt, shame, and the fear of punishment.

Children learn by making a series of efforts and mistakes. The whole process of a child's upbringing and learning is a series of attempts and mistakes until they master some skills. The role of the parents in this process is to provide direction and leadership. You must be a teacher to your children first of all, but a patient one.

The part of the brain that is responsible for reason, logic, and the control of impulses is not fully developed until adolescence. "Immature" behavior is normal in "immature" human beings that have "immature" brains. This is a scientific fact and whatever you feel as a parent and however you behave in these situations, you will not change that.

Parenting is difficult and requires the patience to repeat the same thing hundreds of times. Being a child is also difficult because it requires strength and persistence to repeat the same thing hundreds of times until it is learned. This process cannot be accelerated, skipped, or eliminated. The only thing a parent can do is change their perspective and accept that some things are slow and annoying, and have to be repeated many times. Some parents have days when they feel discouraged because they have to repeat the same thing day after day. But that is also a great part of parenthood.

Children learn about the world from their parents, and learning isn't just about gathering information. One of the most important things in your child's process of learning is learning how to live in the society in which he or she is growing up and learning the rules to function in that society. Kids have to know when it is proper and better for them to limit their autonomy and self-expression and they have to know that they are able to do it. Then, they have to learn how to tolerate frustration and handle frustration and be consistent in spite of it.

Without adequate limits in their environment, children feel agitated and unmanaged. Boundaries can be expressed as criticism and cause embarrassment or they can be uttered in a solid way—full of respect. Think about how you like to be spoken to and speak the same way to your child. Do you respond better to vigorous criticism or to respect, regard, and support? It's the same with your child.

If we allow them to, children will try to solve the problems they face in their development and upbringing. Parents often begin to scold or criticize the child, not expecting the child to attempt to solve the problem. If the parents were more patient, they would be surprised how much their children are actually capable of making conclusions and solving the problems they face.

Being heard is therapeutically powerful and allows us to think about things clearly and find a solution. The same goes for children. Sometimes it's enough just to listen to a child when they talk about the problems they are having because they often come up with solutions that resolve the problems.

Fear and control are effective in the short term, but a child can become either completely blocked in his development or can begin to provide resistance to parental pressure through defiance and rebellion. Depending on the type of interaction a child has with his or her parents, the child forms a picture of himself and a sense of self-reliance in his roles in life. A blocked, non-progressing child has a lesser perception of his value which can lead to isolation or to its opposite: aggressive and rebellious behavior.

Children should understand the importance of thoughts and emotions, not just behavior because it will enable them to function better in relationships with other people and to deal better with problems. That is why adequate control of their emotions is an important skill and one of the most important goals of parenting.

The words of parents and their assessments of a child are a mirror for that child. Children will see what their parents exhibit. That then becomes their picture of themselves and they live with that. That is why it is very important to be specific and accurate with criticism. Criticism should be expressed with body language which expresses regret rather than disapproval toward the child. A parental look full of condemnation and criticism will be internalized by the child, and we want to love and accept our children. This strong support for them will be the seed and the core of their happy life and success.

However, you shouldn't give your child unlimited freedom, you do need to discipline them, of course. But how? Disciplinary measures respond to the child and his abilities and support the child in developing self-discipline. Discipline aims to positively target children, recognizing individual values, and building positive relationships. Positive discipline empowers children's faith in themselves and their ability to behave appropriately.

Discipline is training and orientation that helps children to develop limits, self-control, efficiency, self-sufficiency, and positive social behavior. Discipline is often misunderstood as punishment, especially by those who apply strict punishment in their endeavors to make changes to children's behavior. But discipline is not the same as punishment.

Instead of punishment, it is important for children to be provided with support in the development of self-discipline. Positive discipline shows adults as figures with authority that children give the opportunity to develop strategies to control their own behavior according to the age of the child. Parents should take a positive approach to discipline, developing positive alternatives to punishment.

Education is based on establishing and building relationships with your child, and the basis of each relationship is acceptance, respect, and established boundaries. Setting the boundaries during your child's education is equally important as understanding, love, and support. In this way, children learn to be responsible for what is happening to them, they are helped to learn self-regulation of their feelings and behaviors, and they gain self-confidence, but also to feel the confidence and trust of their parents.

Children are not born with an awareness of what is good and what is not. This is the knowledge that they adopt, and their parents are the ones who assist most in this. It's a tough job and children need the support of adults during this process. Parents just need to learn how to stay patient and calm and help their children to learn in the best way possible.

Tips and Solutions for Peaceful and Positive Parenting
1. Speak in a calm voice—Rather than shout, talk with your child. This will help you to understand how kids need to feel a bit more of your patience. The way you react always influences the way the child behaves. Use positive parenting because it is vital for a healthy relationship between you and your child.

2. Give yourself a break—Patience is time-consuming. Sometimes it's hard to understand why your child behaves in a certain way and what you can do to help them. Patience is difficult when you have no time and your child wants something from you. Patience is the power of understanding your child.

3. Try to understand your child—Understanding is the foundation of positive parenting and influences communication and respect. It is very easy to lose patience with a child you do not understand. Your toddler will always be a little nervous, tearful, angry, or just loud and not listening. However, you're a parent with unconditional love. If you always try to talk to your child from the basis of this unconditional love you will surely understand him better and become more patient.

4. Let your child be independent—If you really want to practice patience, put it to work in situations where you want your child to take on tasks for himself. Stop and allow the child to finish things. This is how the child will enjoy independence and you, at the same time, will learn to be more patient.

5. Find the fastest way to calm yourself down—This is one of the most important things to learn about patience. There are simple things you can do that can help you. For example, deep breathing. You can also count to 10, bake a cake, or something like that. You know what you can do to bring about quick relaxation.

Conclusion

Thank you for reading this book until the end. I hope that it inspires and guides you on your parenting journey.

Remember that parenting is not a marathon or a sprint. It requires time, practice, determination, the right skills, and perseverance to get the golden ticket—a respectful, well-mannered child. It is not a competition that you play with other parents. It is building a personal relationship with your child.

Parenting is about providing loving guidance with great purpose—to mold the character and personality of your child. It is about understanding who he is, what he cares about, what his dreams are, what brings him happiness or sadness, and what are his strengths and weaknesses. It is about focusing your time and attention on what matters to him while keeping limitations and boundaries.

Parenting is also learning about yourself as a nurturer, a disciplinarian, a confidant, and many other roles associated with it. If you make mistakes or feel your patience running out, take a time-out, and relax. You become a fine parent when you are happy, calm, and centered. Your health and well-being matter because it helps you become an objective, affectionate, and positive parent.

By being present and aware, your child is also empowering you and teaching you how to become a better person. When you know who you are, you become more capable of helping him understand himself. And when your child knows himself in the deepest sense, he is more confident to manage the challenges that come his way during his journey to adulthood. He can face the world with excitement and a purpose to contribute positively to make the world a better place to live.

Training kids with positive discipline and giving them a perfect code of living is not an easy task at all. Every kid is different from the other and they have their own understanding of the events as well, although there are some set patterns defined that parents make kids learn. But, the self-understating and evaluation of the matters cause a real difference in their understanding and practice. As parents, it is important to understand that all kids are different and have different needs or interests.

To make your kids grow better and help them with all the good things around them, it is necessary to understand their diversity. Additionally, it is necessary to understand how their needs are different from the others and it is fine to be different. You need to support them in order to construct a better and balanced personality. Imposing the interests and career selections can never be a good option for your kid's brain development.

There should be mutual interests and consultation but the liberty of selection. Your kids need ultimate help from you in the hard times. Their attitude and behavior ask you to look at them and ask the matter not to just punish and put them in detention.

You can identify the important needs of your child and evaluate when, how you can help them with the question, issues, and problems they have. Additionally, you can reconnect them to the humankind and reality of life by cutting them off from the imaginary world of cartoons.

Finally, I wish you good luck for being a wonderful parent who believes that you need tools and guides to bring out the best in your child

www.ingramcontent.com/pod-product-compliance
Lightning Source LLC
Chambersburg PA
CBHW070934080526
44589CB00013B/1516